THE LINCOLNSHIRE WOLDS

BRITAIN IN OLD PHOTOGRAPHS

THE LINCOLNSHIRE
WOLDS

DAVID CUPPLEDITCH

SUTTON PUBLISHING LIMITED

Sutton Publishing Limited
Phoenix Mill · Thrupp · Stroud
Gloucestershire · GL5 2BU

First published 1997

Copyright © David Cuppleditch, 1997

British Library Cataloguing in Publication Data
A catalogue record for this book is available from the
British Library.

ISBN 0-7509-1736-9

Typeset in 10/12 Perpetua.
Typesetting and origination by
Sutton Publishing Limited.
Printed in Great Britain by
Ebenezer Baylis, Worcester.

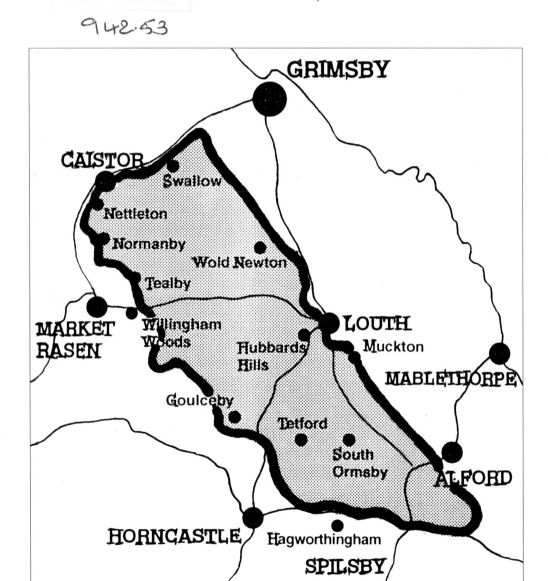

The Lincolnshire Wolds.

CONTENTS

Introduction   7

1.   Alford & Spilsby   9

2.   The Tennyson Legacy   29

3.   Louth & Little Cawthorpe   39

4.   Life on the Wolds   53

5.   Horncastle & Cadwell   77

6.   Some Wold Churches   87

7.   Market Rasen, Binbrook & Caistor   105

Acknowledgements   126

There was a time when dozens of windmills were dotted about the Wolds, but not any more. In 1852 the miller in Binbrook was Thomas Short. His elder son, William, followed in his father's footsteps and became a miller, while George, the youngest son, became a baker! The windmill was situated at the end of Mount Pleasant (now a Council estate) and slightly proud of the village.

INTRODUCTION

Lincolnshire's great secret lies in the Wolds. This rolling undulation, which is more gentle than its near rival and more famous Yorkshire Dales, is mostly unappreciated and yet remains Lincolnshire's great strength.

There are parts of the Wolds where time seems to have stood still for the last hundred years and visitors could find themselves walking in exactly the same landscape as that of the last century. Impressive skies which appear over the Wolds are particularly memorable and range from an ominous black on rainy days to a rainbow selection of sunsets, especially in winter, with every variant in between. It was along these windy roads and deserted fields that T.E. Lawrence found solace when he enrolled at RAF Cranwell; he wanted to hide away from the world and the media of his day. Taking his trusty motorbike (a Brough Superior from Nottingham), he travelled unimpeded through the Wolds to seek inspiration for his book *The Revolt in the Desert* (the abridged version of *The Seven Pillars of Wisdom*), which he completed in Lincoln.*

Lincolnshire is divided up into three administrative parts, known as Kesteven, Holland and Lindsey. The Wolds come into the latter region and rise to a height of 548 ft above sea level. The modern misconception of Lincolnshire as being flat, which still exists today, often confuses anyone who lives on the Wolds.

Curiously enough, there has never been a book written specifically about the Lincolnshire Wolds, although James Hissey's journey through the southern part of the Wolds is described in his book *Over Fen and Wold* (1898). Hissey's meanderings turned into a quest for Tennyson's imaginary Locksley Hall. What he found were bits of Locksley scattered about, such as 'Yonder in that chapel slowly sinking now into the ground' – a reference to Harrington Church, which was indeed sinking into the ground in Tennyson's day. The incumbent, the Revd Mr Cracroft, was responsible for saving the church. 'Here is Locksley Hall, my grandson, here the lion guarded gate' is a clear reference to the lion gateway of Scrivelsby. But Tennyson always maintained that both of his poems, 'Locksley Hall' and 'Locksley Hall Sixty Years After', were a compilation of ideas and remembrances rather than any specific place.

In 1851 there were many farmers on the Lincolnshire Wolds who were tenants of 2,000 acres or more – as much land as some squires might own. There was also a marked difference between these farmers and their agricultural labourers, whose average weekly wage was 11s! In the latter part of the century wages improved but even so farm labourers could barely afford home comforts. Often their furniture was of cheap pine (which has recently become fashionable again) and lighting by paraffin lamp.

Although we know the Wolds for its Lincoln Red cattle and Longwool sheep, Lincolnshire was also the home of the early bone-crushing industry. It is sad to think that these early fertilizers should have advanced so much these days that they have become detrimental rather than beneficial. Crushed bones or bone dust were a source of phosphate and nitrogen when applied as a top dressing on light land soils. It worked well too!

Running through the middle of the Wolds is the old Bluestone Heath Road where there are some tranquil views, such as the view from Red Hill (now a nature reserve) near Stenigot or the view from Flint Hill near Scamblesby.

It is not surprising that many famous people have been born on the Wolds – from Sarah Jennings (the first Duke of Marlborough's wife), who was born at Burwell Manor, to Sir Joseph Banks (the botanist), who was born at Revesby. In this century, Basil Boothroyd, who later became literary editor of *Punch*, worked for some time at a bank in Horncastle before following his literary aspirations, and Bernie Taupin (Elton John's lyricist) went to school at Market Rasen Comprehensive.

There has always been the photographer's eagle eye on hand to record events and life in general. It is no wonder this chalk-capped area has been designated an area of outstanding natural beauty, as ramblers or travellers have found. It remains a peaceful haven for anyone wanting to escape the hectic hustle and bustle of everyday life and long may it continue.

* Lawrence joined the RAF in 1922 under the name of Aircraftsman Ross. After a few months the press got hold of the story and he was dismissed. He then changed his name to Shaw and joined the Tank Corps. After a year he managed to get a transfer to the RAF. He arrived in Cranwell in August 1925 and on occasions spent the night in a lodging house at 33 Steep Hill, Lincoln. The lodging house was kept by a Mrs Dugdale who recalled that one night Lawrence had driven a long distance on his motorcycle in the pouring rain. Mrs Dugdale had a meal ready and said to Lawrence, 'Now just go to the sink and wash your hands and face before you sit down.' 'Good heavens, woman,' said Lawrence, 'God's been washing my face all the way here!' Lawrence left Cranwell for India at the end of 1926.

Before the advent of photography visual images were limited to prints, paintings and engravings. This engraving showed the remains of one of the two ruinous gateways left within the grounds of Belleau Manor. The name of Belleau is derived from the copious spring water which originated here, and Belleau Manor was the home of Sir Henry Vane (1613–62), one-time Governor of Massachusetts (1636–7), MP for Hull and author of *The Retired Man's Meditations*. He was executed in the reign of Charles II.

ALFORD & SPILSBY

This aerial view of Alford shows the Market Place and, to the right, St Wilfrid's Church, which Sir Gilbert Scott restored in 1867–8. Alford obtained its Market Charter in 1283 when William de Welle was Lord of the Manor of Alford.

This was West Street in Edwardian times, with some old thatched cottages on the left in front of the Methodist Chapel.

Wesley's brand of Methodism swept through Lincolnshire like a tidal wave, and in this photograph, showing the Lincolnshire Yeomanry in the Market Place, the sign 'Alford Wesleyan Sunday School' is more prominent than anything else.

The view looking back up West Street.

The White Horse Hotel which dates back to the 1600s is on the left-hand side.

Alford is one of the few towns left in Lincolnshire to retain a working windmill. Known as Hoyles' Mill, it was built in 1813 by Sam Oxley and fully restored in 1979 by Mr C. Davis. Here we see a group of Morris men performing at the foot of the mill.

The Windmill Inn in the Market Place (or the Commercial Hotel and Posting House, as it was known) owes its name to a mill, although it is unlikely to have been Hoyles' Mill as the mill depicted here has six sails. Instead it is more likely to be one of the three other Alford windmills, now demolished. It was here at the old Windmill Inn that Thomas Paine established his office as Excise Officer in 1764, a post he held until he was dismissed in 1765. Thomas Paine (1737–1809) wrote two important books, *The Rights of Man* and *The Age of Reason*, and was responsible for preparing the American colonies for independence.

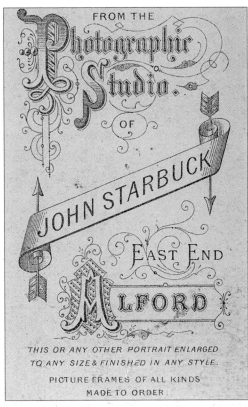

The earliest recorded photographer in Alford was John Starbuck, of East End.

This carte-de-visite portrait of an attractive young woman is an example of his work.

Starbuck's successor, Edwin Nainby, was prolific. This was one of Nainby's studies of the King George V Jubilee celebrations, 1935. It shows Alford Town Band with Russell Barnes as bandmaster and part of the procession in the Market Place. Incidentally, the shop to let in the background was taken over by International Stores.

In the Edwardian golden age, postcards such as this one abounded.

This view of the Market Place looks a bit empty, suggesting, perhaps, that the photograph was taken on a Sunday.

South Market Place, again on a Sunday, perhaps.

Alford has always been noted for its Bull Fair, usually held on the first Thursday in November. This photograph of the auction was taken in 1955.

One of the prize bulls.

Sadly, like so many other cattle markets in Lincolnshire, Alford's cattle market diminished in the '60s and '70s until it was forced to close in 1987.

Another casualty in Alford has been the War Memorial Hospital, shut in the upheavals of a muddled present-day NHS. The Alford War Memorial Hospital was opened by the Countess of Yarborough in August 1921 in memory of the men from Alford and District who fell in the First World War.

Here we see Remembrance Day in 1955, when Lieutenant D.W. Newsum (Alford Battalion, Royal Lincolnshire Regiment) laid a wreath.

On a lighter note, there were children's parties during the '50s. On this occasion, the pastor is entertaining the children with his Archie Andrews lookalike puppet.

More recently Alford has been revitalized with the craft market. Initially designed by Michael and Heather Ducos for craft exhibitions, it now runs on a regular commercial basis. Here a thatcher demonstrates the almost lost art of thatching.

Bob Oakes, the smithy of Alvingham, demonstrating some ironmongery.

Just a short distance away from Alford is Well Vale. Long the home of the Rawnsley family (the last Mrs Rawnsley died in 1978), in more recent times it was owned by Mr Reeve who preferred to live in a smaller modern house within the grounds rather than at the hall. The hall is currently owned by Maypole School which was founded in 1884 in Horncastle.

The grounds and lake are peaceful, as can be seen in this photograph.

Not far from Alford and nestling neatly on the edge of the Wolds is the small market town of Spilsby, with a statue of John Franklin dominating the western side of the Market Place.

Sir John Franklin (1786–1847), the Spilsby-born Arctic explorer, spent two years at Louth Grammar School before joining the Navy at the age of fourteen. He saw action at the Battle of Copenhagen in 1801, and two months later was appointed midshipman under another Lincolnshire man, Captain Matthew Flinders. During an illustrious career in the Navy, his ultimate achievement was to be credited with discovering the North-West Passage. His body was never found.

At the turn of the century A. Greetham was the saddler, but his business days were numbered as the age of motor traffic loomed on the horizon.

Aware of the possibilities of this new form of transport was J.A. Badley. His business as cycle agent and motor car dealer was operated from The Terrace, which was near Main Road, Spilsby.

On the east side of the Market Place is Spilsby's famous Market Cross, dating back originally to the fourteenth century.

Although Edwin Nainby had a photograpic studio in Spilsby, the main photographer in the town was T. Bundock of the Market Place.

During the First World War the 5th Lincolns had an OC training camp at Spilsby. Here we see Colonel Beaumont Walker enjoying some refreshment between sorties.

Captain Bell and Major Marshall (with his Field Marshal Haig stance).

A group of young officers of 'B' Company.

There was little time to take photographs in those hectic days of the First World War except in moments of relaxation. I wonder if these two had any idea of what they would walk into when they went on active service?

Of the many fine houses that surrounded Spilsby only a handful are left, including Dalby Hall. The original Hall was destroyed by fire in the eighteenth century and the new Hall was built in 1856 to the designs of James Fowler, of Louth.

Dalby Hall should not be confused with Dalby Grange, the home of Peter Middleton, which is a farmhouse in the old-fashioned sense of the word.

Another fine house in the Spilsby area is Revesby Abbey, which escaped demolition only by a whisker. This house was built on the site of Sir Joseph Banks' house, which in turn was built on the site of the Abbot's House of Revesby Abbey. Remains of the old Cistercian abbey have long since disappeared.

This is the author standing in the porch just outside the front entrance in 1974 to give the reader some idea of size. This enormous pile was built in the 1840s by J. Banks-Stanhope and since the early 1960s has been left unoccupied and derelict.

The old East Lincolnshire Railway line carefully skirted the Wolds. On the east side from Boston to Grimsby it went through Sibsey, Old Leake, East Ville, Little Steeping and Firsby, looping around Willoughby, Alford, Aby, Authorpe, Legbourne and Louth before straightening up for Grimsby. This was Firsby Junction, where it was possible to change for Spilsby, in 1954.

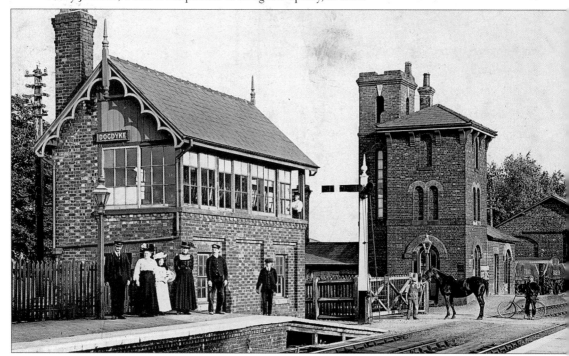

The other line from Boston to Lincoln went through Langrick, Dogdyke, Tattershall, Woodhall, Kirkstead (change for Horncastle), Stixwould, Southrey and Bardney on its way to Lincoln. This was Dogdyke station at the turn of the century.

THE TENNYSON LEGACY

Alfred Tennyson was born on 6 August 1809 at Somersby Rectory, the fourth of twelve children of the then rector, George Clayton Tennyson, and his wife, Elizabeth, a daughter of Stephen Fytche, vicar of Louth.

George Clayton Tennyson (sometimes referred to as the Doctor) was rector of Somersby and Bag Enderby churches. During Tennyson's time at Somersby, the roof of the church was thatched, but was subsequently tiled in one of the two nineteenth-century restorations.

It was here that the young Alfred Lord Tennyson was baptised and, as a boy, helped to toll the bell.

In the graveyard, Tennyson was reputed to have scratched the words 'Byron is dead' on a rock in 1824, close by the fifteenth-century cross.

Dr Tennyson's other church of Bag Enderby was more spartan than Somersby, but he livened it up with remarkable sermons. One local was heard to remark: 'E read 'em from a paaper and I didn't know what 'e meant.' George Clayton Tennyson had taken his degree as a Doctor of Civil Law in 1813.

Reminders of Alfred Tennyson's time in Somersby abound, such as 'The Brook', depicted romantically on this postcard.

This photograph of the babbling brook is vastly different from the brook that is left today. (Incidentally, Tennyson's famous poem 'The Brook' had to be rescued from the wastepaper bin!)

Stockwith Mill (on the road to Hagworthingham) still survives as a tea-room and gift shop. Local gossip has it that the mill inspired Tennyson's poem 'The Miller's Daughter' but I can find no evidence of this. Indeed, references in 'The Miller's Daughter' point to Hubbard's Hills' windmill (now demolished). There was a watermill less than a hundred yards away, which ground flour on days when there wasn't enough wind. 'Where this old mansion mounted high looks down upon the village spire' was more likely to be Thorpe Hall and 'The white chalk-quarry from the Hill' could either have been Hubbard's Hills or the quarry just off London Road.

Other pieces of Tennyson memorabilia, such as this thatched cottage in Bag Enderby, have gone.

The woodcutter's cottage still survives, echoing a timeless reminder that much of the countryside around this area has changed little in the last 150 years.

Next to Somersby Rectory is the Vanbrugh creation of Somersby Grange. This family group was photographed by Edwin Nainby of Alford in about 1900.

Another village with Tennyson connections is Tealby. It is here that the River Rase comes fresh from its source at Bully Hill.

It was also here that Charles Tennyson d'Eyncourt (Alfred Tennyson's uncle) built Bayons Manor on the site of the old manor in 1830. Imposing and solid as it was, with castellated battlements, Bayons Manor was eventually blown up with dynamite in the mid-1960s.

The grandiose setting of Charles Tennyson d'Eyncourt's Bayons Manor is further demonstrated in this photograph of moat, drawbridge and portcullis! In 1807 a labourer discovered an earthenware pot containing 6,000 Henry II silver pennies while ploughing a field on the Tennyson estate. Some of the coins ended up in the British Museum.

Charles Tennyson (Alfred's elder brother) was vicar of Grasby for about forty years. Grasby lies on the western edge of the Wolds with some fine views of Caistor and beyond. Charles Tennyson arrived in Grasby in 1835 as Charles Tennyson Turner, after succeeding to the estate of his great-uncle, Samuel Turner of Caistor. In 1837 he was joined in Grasby by his young wife Louisa, a niece of Sir John Franklin and sister of Emily Sellwood, later to become Alfred Tennyson's wife.

A rare photograph of Lady Tennyson d'Eyncourt addressing a group of girl scouts in Louth in the late '20s. She accepted the invitation from Mrs Oscar Dixon of Abbey House, Louth.

This would have been Alfred Tennyson's first view of Louth as he travelled along the London Road to attend Louth Grammar School. The gradient of the road would have been a little steeper in his day. It was Napoleonic prisoners of war who hacked out the chalk to lower the road (in about 1810 to 1815), so making the journey less perilous for stagecoaches and horse-drawn carts.

Although the group of Louth Grammar School boys in School House Lane was photographed in 1860, it would not have differed greatly from any group in Tennyson's day.

LOUTH &
LITTLE CAWTHORPE

Louth has sometimes been referred to as the capital of the Wolds. Much of its wealth originally came from wool, and farmers have used it as a trade centre for the last 500 years. Here we see the cattle market in about 1905.

Although the cattle market is no longer the bustling, busy centre that it was, there are still auctions and a Christmas stock show. Dennis and Stephen Nundy of Lincross are showing off their champion 'beast' in this photograph.

The Union Workhouse, or 'Poorhouse', as it was known locally, was built in 1837 to house 300 paupers. It is now Louth County Hospital, but many people of the older generation were reluctant to use it because of its past connotations. A Louth woman, Mrs Janetta Norwebb, who died in Brigg Poorhouse in 1817, numbered among her most intimate acquaintances Laurence Sterne, the author of *Tristram Shandy*.

The Louth Volunteers were formed in 1814. This photograph of a group of sergeants by Plumtree was taken in about 1870.

Even at the turn of the century, after the Boer War, the Volunteers were still going strong. They often met at the Cow Pastures or the rifle range (commonly known as 'The Butts') off the South Elkington road. The Volunteers eventually amalgamated with Louth Rifle Club.

Carved out of the Wolds by the River Lud is a natural beauty spot known as Hubbard's Hills (it was called Hubbard's Valley in Victorian times). Even when this photograph was taken, in about 1890, it served as a peaceful haven.

Just a short distance from Hubbard's Hills is the tollbar on the Horncastle Road. The 1770 Tolls Act allowed for charges to be made for horse-drawn traffic. There were certain exceptions, such as the Royal Mail, clergy visiting the sick, or people attending a church service or worship.

In the early part of this century the tollbar house was the home of Bill Cribb (1902–47). He was the son of Mr Cribb the solicitor, whose office was above Strawson's shop in the Market Place.

Of all the photographers working in Louth probably the most prolific was Arthur James of Ramsgate House. This delightful 'Lincolnshire worthy' was photographed in about 1880.

This Victorian couple have obviously donned their best clothes for the photograph.

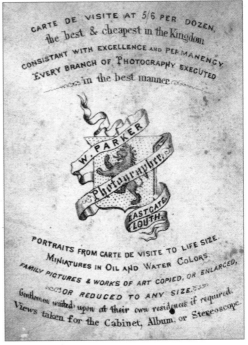

The back of W. Parker's carte-de-visite.

This was the reverse of Arthur James' carte-de-visite, showing his premises in Ramsgate, which were sadly demolished by the flood in 1920.

In the last century Louth had three firms of coachbuilders, Thorn's, Richardson's and Esberger's. This was
Esberger's bill depicting their comprehensive selection of carriages.

Although overshadowed by the more famous boys' school, King Edward VI Girls' Grammar School has also produced a selection of notable old girls, sometimes forgotten in the wake of their husbands' illustrious careers. Here we see the tennis team of 1911 comprising from left to right, G. Wright, L. Southern, R. Smith and E. Bach.

Nor did the girls just stick to tennis: this was the cricket team of 1911! Back row, left to right: S. Yates, M. Oldroyd, Nora Lane, Rose Robinson, Mabel ?, -?-. Front row: Miss Millson, A. Wright, Miss M. Millson, Miss Marshall and P. Taylor.

Here we see the Bank Holiday meet of the Southwold Hunt in the Cornmarket, Louth, in 1954.

It is the Boxing Day meet of the Southwold Hunt at the cattle market that sticks in my mind. This was one of the highlights of the year and a fixed date in many people's calendars, reliving the century-old tradition.

Just a short distance away from Louth is Little Cawthorpe, with its manor house and pub, the Royal Oak (nicknamed The Splash by many locals). The village was awarded the title of Best Kept Small Village in Lincolnshire in 1988.

Between Little Cawthorpe and Legbourne is Watery Lane, which was a short-cut in Edwardian times. Here we see Cornelius Potts (taxi driver from the Mason's Arms) navigating the shallow stream in his pony and trap.

This is the source of the Great Eau, and it was possibly for dogcarts and even motor cars to drive down it. This photograph dates from about 1926.

Life was hard in Edwardian times and many local residents of Little Cawthorpe had to look to the land for sustenance. Here we see old Mrs Barton, who kept chickens at one end of Watery Lane.

Mr James Barton, the postman, outside his house in Cawthorpe.

Here we see a Conservative Party raffle in front of the Jacobean manor house. The photo was taken in the '50s with the Revd Mr Swaby (who wrote *A History of Louth*) on the extreme left. In the centre of the photograph is the late Cyril Osborne, MP for Louth, with Mr Nielson (in spectacles) immediately behind him.

Cawthorpe Manor bears the crest of the ill-fated Mottram family, who were wiped out by smallpox. Inside the house (this is the drawing room) is a rich array of carved woodwork, some of which may have come from nearby Legbourne Abbey after the Dissolution of the Monasteries. For more than a century it was the family home of the Mortons who, among other things, trained one of Edward VIII's racehorses during the early part of this century. Then it became the family home of the Nielsons before the current owners, Mr and Mrs Charles Grant and family, moved in.

The pond, just in front of the Manor House, made a tranquil picture.

LIFE ON THE WOLDS

Life on the Wolds at the turn of the century was hard in many respects, yet it had its rewards. Most families 'made do' with their slim resources, and couples who had their photographs taken liked to be seen in their Sunday best.

There was little crime and if the police had to be contacted the matter was obviously serious. This smart police station sergeant was photographed in about 1870.

The stereotype of Wold life was captured in this view of a milkmaid in Old Bolingbroke. It portrays a serene, almost idyllic way of life.

Even in the '50s it was possible to tour the Wolds in relative seclusion. Here we see Sophus Nielson of Welton Manor stopping by the roadside to enjoy the scenery.

The agricultural year culminated in the harvest festival. This splendid array of produce in the old South Elkington Church Hall dates from about 1900.

Carts or wagons were used to transport hay or crops.

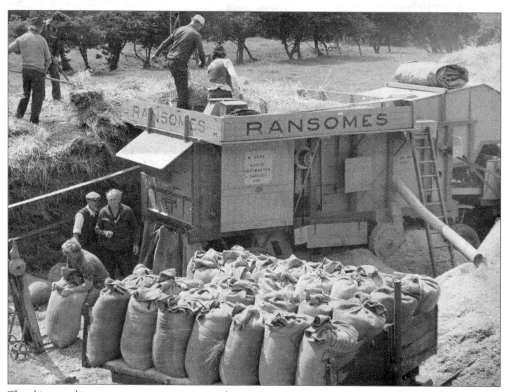

Threshing machines were put into operation at harvest.

This delightful photograph of Tom Barton, the Ludford butcher, with his son Arthur, was taken in about 1903. The Bartons lived at Ivy House, Ludford.

During the First World War there were country shoots. This photograph, of about 1916, was taken in the Binbrook/Rothwell area.

Alternatively there was rabbiting. This was C. ('Gyp') Parker photographed in 1914 with his sack on his back.

Up to the First World War, most people viewed the Wolds via pony and trap. The horse in this photograph is Mustang.

The advances in automobility saw a new mode of transport, the motorcycle, sometimes with side-car, such as this brand new Indian in 1915.

Corn stooks lined the fields in the inter-war years on the Wolds.

At this Conservative dinner in the late '30s we can see the familiar figure of Major J. St Vigor-Fox (in grey suit), fourth from right. He was High Steward of Louth and lived at Girsby Manor. Next to him (the smaller gentleman, third from the right) is Lieutenant Colonel A.P. Heneage MP, who came from Hainton Hall but lived for most of his life at nearby Walesby Hall.

Girsby Manor was demolished after a Mr Holmes of Wragby bought the house and stripped it of its wood and lead. Subsequently it became unsafe and had to be knocked down.

Hainton Hall, where the Heneage family had lived for generations, did not fare too well either, although at least most of it is still standing. A large chunk of it was altered when dry rot was discovered in the '50s.

There were, and still are, a selection of village pubs to visit, such as the Blue Bell, Belchford (seen here), near Horncastle, but these were the days before the drink-drive laws came into force.

The White Hart, Tetford, dates from about 1520 and it was here that the famous Dr Johnson reputedly drank. Other village pubs that spring to mind are the Three Horseshoes, Goulceby, the Durham Ox, Thimbleby, the Sebastopol, Minting, the Nickerson Arms, Rothwell, the King's Head, Tealby, and the Vine, South Thoresby.

Farming methods were to change in the post-Second World War era. Here we see Bill Massey, Ralph Baumber and George Hallgarth in front of their first combine harvester at Driby in 1955.

Many people still hankered after the old way of life. This splendid photograph of Harold Baldock with his twenty-one-year-old mare, Judy, was taken as late as 1996. He is seen ploughing his farm at North Willingham.

The post-war advance in farming meant that there was much crop-spraying to increase yield. This is a field of barley. It is only recently that we have come to understand that perhaps the old way of farming was best, as more and more people turn to organic foods.

Had farmers or the financial institutions that own farms stuck to more conventional methods the nation would be a lot healthier. There was nothing wrong with those old labour-intensive methods: harvesting in 1956 is seen here.

Artificial fertilizers have done much damage to the land and even more damage to the NHS, as puzzled doctors find new ailments caused either directly or indirectly by these chemicals. Clues only came to light after crop-spraying aeroplanes went off course and sprayed people rather than crops.

Whether harvesting was worth taking to this extreme is questionable. Gluts in production, owing to over-generous subsidies, often meant that Britain landed up with grain mountains. This meant that Britain fed Russia or Poland or some obscure country just to use up the excess before it went mouldy. But at least the price was kept high!

Atrocities committed in the post-war era in the name of progress could only be put down to greed. The sign on this snow-covered field is self-explanatory.

If chemicals hit the vegetable crop, with any overspill of effluent entering the water supply, there was even worse to come with BSE (or mad cow disease). Here we see a Lincoln Red heifer and her calf.

In this photograph the Lincoln Red Cattle Society are safely perched on a hayrick well out of reach of the cattle.

To keep cattle in, a series of cattle grids were built in the '50s and '60s. Here we see a typical cattle grid being built at Driby with, from left to right, Phil Olivant, John Mountain, Jim Roper and George Hallgarth.

Occasionally there were farming demonstrations to show the machines that replaced horsepower in the 1970s. Did they reassure farmers that they were adopting the right attitudes? The International Junior pictured here was a throwback to a bygone age.

I'm not sure the farmers shown here were entirely convinced as they studied a tractor going through its paces.

One great character was the late Eric Ranby of Grimblethorpe Hall, born at Bilsby Hall near Alford. He was a fiercely independent farmer whose actions sometimes bordered on the eccentric.

Electricity did not reach some Wold villages until after the Second World War. Here we see an electricity van in Thoresway off to repair a broken cable. Before the advent of the electric light, candles were used for lighting and open fires for heat. On the left is the old wheelhouse with its water wheel which has long since been dormant. An amazing AA sign on the side of the wheelhouse states that Thoresby is 155¼ miles from London! Farmers frequently had to harness a stream or running water to create energy to run their threshing machines. The barn in this case was on the other side of the road, and a shaft was built beneath the road to drive the threshing machine. It was built in 1813 and last used in the 1930s.

Because the Wolds are so undulating many dips and hollows are prone to flooding. Here we see a lorry negotiating the road out of North Willingham, which is awash with rainwater.

Lincolnshire is well known for its huntin', shootin' and fishin' set. Here we see two local squires: Will Haggas of the Walmsgate estate (left) and David Haxby of Ketsby.

Another possible sport or pastime which may become a thing of the past is fox-hunting. Here we see the South Wold Hunt going through Welton-le-Wold on their Boxing Day Meet.

Two adamant and aggressive Anti-Hunt League protestors questioning the morality of fox-hunting.

Another sight that we shall see no more – stubble burning; it was banned in 1994!

One or two villages have adopted the word 'wold' into their names, such as Welton-le-Wold. This is Welton Vale (the road leading to Welton-le-Wold), *c.* 1900.

Walton Vale, Louth.

Other villages such as Wold Newton or Barnetby-le-Wold (seen here) have acquired a wold attachment to separate them from other villages of the same name.

There are many villages and towns with the suffix 'thorpe' or 'by' from Lincolnshire's time under Danelaw. In the northern part of the Wolds the name of Thor appears as a prefix quite regularly, as in North Thoresby, Thorganby, Thoresway and Thornton-le-Moor. In Norse mythology Thor was the patron god of peasants and the lower classes (he was also their god of thunder!). This delightful photograph of Thoresway was taken in the '50s.

Basically the Lincolnshire Wolds comprise farmers and their produce. This is the weekly auction held in the Cornmarket, Louth, under the watchful gaze of auctioneer Charles Thompson.

These four spring onions, grown by Walter Phillips of Barnetby, are fine examples of home-grown produce. The judge Geoffrey Houltby (right) is accompanied by steward Archie Eastcrabbe and his assistant Brian Wood.

Here we see Mrs A. Heneage (wife of the Louth MP Colonel Heneage) at the Conservative Horse Show of 1933, which was held at North Thoresby. She presented the prizes.

HORNCASTLE & CADWELL

Horncastle once had the biggest horse-fair in the country, and George Borrow refers to a horsey connection in the town in his book The Romany Rye *of 1857.*

The Bull Ring had a healthy cluster of hostelries surrounding it.

St Mary's Church is neatly hidden away. This view of it from St Mary's Square was taken by W.K. Morton. During the Civil War Cavalier Sir Ingram Hopton was buried in this church on Cromwell's instructions, after he had been killed at the Battle of Winceby.

At the turn of the century Horncastle comprised many small cottages often with pantiled roofs, as can be seen in this selection off Spilsby Road.

There was a marked contrast between the workers' cottages and the larger more ornate country houses such as Baumber Park. Before the First World War this was owned by the Sharpe family.

A couple of miles outside Horncastle lies Scrivelsby, the ancestral home of the Kings' Champion, whose role is to defend the monarch's right to the throne against challenges. This feudal tradition, once held by the Marmions, is continued to this day by the Dymoke family. This is the Lion gateway, in about 1925.

The name of Marmion is still retained in the Marmion Arms at Haltham.

The original Scrivelsby Court, ancient home of the Dymokes, caught fire in the reign of George III and most of the old manor, including the great hall, was destroyed. This photograph shows the later Manor, which fell into disrepair and was demolished in the 1950s, leaving the present Dymokes to live in a conversion of one of the gatehouses of the original Scivelsby Court.

Just a short distance away from Scrivelsby (between Dalderby and Scrivelsby) lay this unique cottage known as Tea Pot Hall. It burned down in 1945. The photograph was taken by Hugh Martineau, who took many of the photographs in this book.

The late Hugh Martineau was a schoolmaster by profession. He taught at St Hugh's School, Woodhall Spa for over twenty years, where his nickname was far from complimentary. Latterly he can be remembered for his many contributions to *Lincolnshire Life* both as a writer and as a photographer.

The most recent event to capture the public's attention was the World Ploughing Championships, which were held just outside Horncastle in 1984.

A view of the ploughing parade marching through the town, September 1984.

Everyone who attended the event needed feeding, but it was unrecorded whether these three were eating a ploughman's!

Formerly known as Cadwell Vale, it was here that Cadwell Hall once stood – until it was demolished in 1921. The grounds of the estate became a motorcycle track in 1934, the brainchild of the Wilkinson family.

Cadwell Hall was the country seat of the Allenby family, and was where General Edmund Henry Hynman Allenby (1861–1936) was born. He had two uncles who were landowners in the area, Everitt Allenby of Fotherby and Hynman Allenby of Kenwick Hall, and an aunt who lived in George Street, Louth.

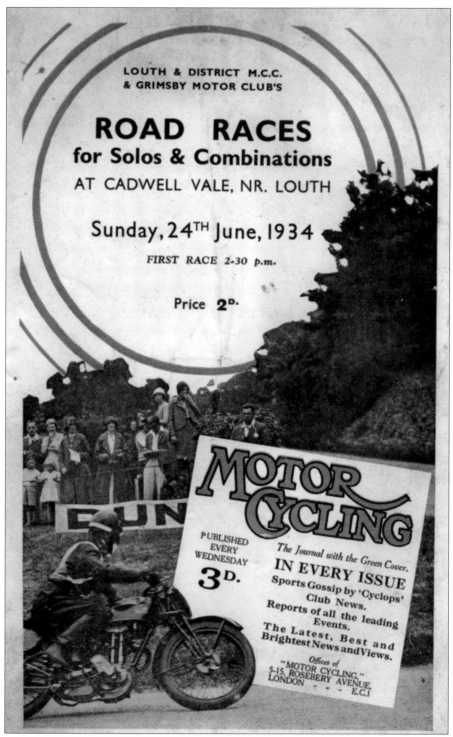

Cadwell Vale soon became a popular venue with local motorcycle enthusiasts and, more recently, world champions such as Mike Hailwood, Barry Sheene, Giacomo Agostini, Wayne Gardner and Roger Marshall have ridden on this circuit.

Cadwell Park is well known throughout Europe for its motorcycle races. This photograph, of about 1955, shows just how popular this sport had become.

Cadwell Park is not just confined to motorcycles, as can be seen in this photograph of two vintage cars going around the track.

SOME WOLD CHURCHES

St Olave's, Ruckland, was practically rebuilt in 1885 from designs by architect W. Scorer at a cost of £400. There is a distinctive rose window in the west wall.

The Revd George Hall (1863–1918) was vicar
at St Olave's, Ruckland, from 1905 to 1918.
He wrote *The Gypsy Parson*, published in 1915
by Sampson Low Marston & Co.

All Saints' Church, Haugham, was
modelled on St James' Church, Louth, and
its spire can be very confusing, especially
when driving to Louth on the A16 from
Boston: it is such a good replica that many a
traveller has muddled the two spires. This
photograph was taken in about 1870.

Although largely redundant the church is still occasionally used, as can be seen at this baptism of 1993.

St Vedast's, Tathwell, was named after the sixth-century French bishop, and much of the Norman building was retained in the 1889 restoration. The obelisk to the right of the photograph is a monument to Lord William Henry Cavendish Bentinck (1804–70), one of the sons of the fourth Duke of Portland.

The Hamby memorial inside is an imposing monument of alabaster erected in 1627, depicting William Hamby kneeling at a desk and Edward and Elizabeth Hamby at another desk below. Jean Howard, curator of Louth Museum and a champion of old memorials, is standing in the foreground of the photograph.

At Raithby-with-Hallington, snugly tucked into the foothills of the Wolds, is the delightful church of St Peter. It was completely rebuilt in 1839 by the Revd Henry Chaplin at his own expense, although the beautiful fourteenth-century font was retained. The Revd Mr Nunnally was rector of Raithby from 1959 to 1978.

This delightful setting of St Mary's Church, Harrington, shows the tower peeping over the trees. It is reached by the road, not by the Hall! Harrington Hall was rebuilt by the Amcotts family in 1673 on the medieval foundations of the old Coppledick family seat. It was also here that Tennyson was inspired to write 'Come into the garden, Maud', dedicated to Rosa Baring (a member of the eminent banking family), who lived at Harrington for a number of years.

St John the Baptist Church, Belleau, was another church almost completely rebuilt in 1862 while retaining its medieval font. The original church on this site was built by Ralph West of Claythorpe between 1307 and 1327.

Some Wold churches have fared better than others. When I last visited All Saints', Oxcombe, the church was in a poor state of repair with notices warning of falling masonry.

Holy Trinity, Muckton, may have been demolished, but these two delightful photographs remain of Mrs Surgey, wife of the vicar. Herbert Henry Surgey was the incumbent from 1905 to 1914.

This delightful photograph taken of Mrs Surgey was taken in the rectory grounds.

St Michael's Church, Driby, could easily have gone the same way, but has since been converted into a Gothic revival private residence by London barrister Keith Walmsley.

There are many fine examples of fonts in Lincolnshire churches. The octagonal font in Bag Enderby church with its representations of the Pieta – Christ's mother holding on her knees the body of her son taken from the cross – a seated figure with a lute and a fox, part of Lincolnshire folklore.

All Saints' Church, Hameringham, 3½ miles from Horncastle. The name Hameringham means village on the hill and the church contains a Jacobean pulpit with the original hourglass in its stand – presumably to remind the vicar not to preach too long!

The village of Burwell was once a busy market town. This photograph of it was taken in the '50s, showing the butter cross in the far distance. The church of St Michael is a short distance away from the village.

About the only reminder of Burwell's importance is the old red-brick butter cross, which served as a dovecote for a number of years and is now used as a church hall.

Here we see Mrs Surgey (once again) and Mrs Watson standing outside the entrance to Burwell Church.

This more modern photograph shows the Revd Peter Fluck (brother of the late Diana Dors) inspecting an old door. Peter Fluck was rector of the South Ormsby group of churches from 1975 to 1984.

Mr Fluck was a resourceful and down-to-earth cleric who will long be remembered in this area for holding services in the Massingberd Arms pub! Many so-called Christian vicars may take note; it's not the church or material surroundings that matter but Christian principles, thought and conscience that should be paramount in a service of worship.

The delightful church of St Andrew in Donington on Bain has changed little since this photograph was taken in about 1910.

The church at Thoresway near Binbrook, which had an idyllic setting, has had the indignity of a modern house built just to the right of this photograph, in front of the church.

At least it has fared better than Calceby church. All that is left of the Church of St Andrew, which is mentioned in the Domesday Book, are these few stones. The last service was held in this church in about 1692.

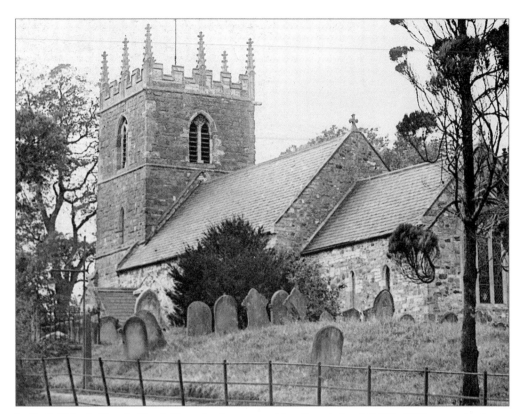

Inside St Helen's Church, North Thoresby, is a memorial to Francis Bond (1850–1918), an authority on church architecture, fonts and woodcarving, who was born in North Thoresby.

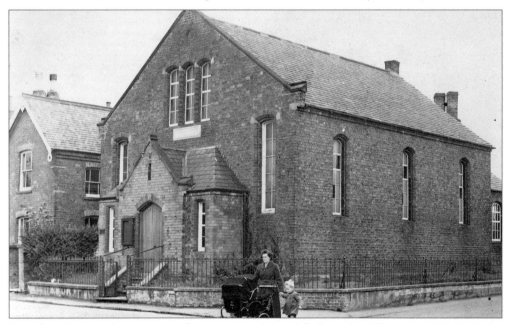

As well as churches, there are many fine examples of chapels still standing. This is the 1846 Methodist Chapel at North Thoresby, but other examples can be found throughout the county.

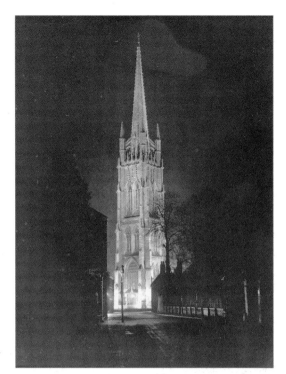

Probably the most impressive parish church in the Wolds is St James', Louth, seen here in 1934. It has the tallest parish church spire in England and is one of the few parishes to have had its vicar hanged, drawn and quartered. Thomas Kendall suffered this fate for his part in the Lincolnshire Rising of 1536.

Here we see Owen Price, long-time organist of St James' (1897–1946), choirmaster and music teacher. The photograph was taken on 4 April 1940.

All Saints', Walesby, has often been nicknamed 'the ramblers' church' because of its situation. Among the list of former rectors is the name of the Revd R. Burton, author of *The Anatomy of Melancholy* – just the sort of book to cheer up any worn-out rambler!

Another Wold church with RAF connections is Ludford. It is yet another James Fowler-designed church, and like Binbrook St Mary and St Peter is a combination of two previous churches, which once served Ludford Parva and Ludford Magna.

To commemorate the crew of Lancaster PB476, No. 12 Squadron, RAF Wickenby, a small stone memorial was unveiled by Trevor Budworth (of the Lincolnshire Military Preservation Society) and Padre Ivor Haythorne. There are many such memorials honouring the RAF dotted about the Wolds, often by the roadside.

The delightful church of St Mary and St Gabriel in Binbrook stands as a tribute to that prolific Victorian architect James Fowler. Two previous churches combined to make one, and it was consecrated in 1869. Inside there is a stained glass window commemorating its close ties with RAF Binbrook.

MARKET RASEN, BINBROOK & CAISTOR

Looking down King Street, Market Rasen, at the turn of the century. The Greyhound Inn (one of the oldest pubs in the area, established in 1639) on the left of the photo advertises 'stabling or billiards together with Ind Coope's ales and stouts delivered in cask and bottle'.

The Greyhound, in the late '50s or early '60s. The photograph shows that the pub had become a café! It is now known as The Chase.

Market Rasen has a good golf course and excellent tennis club. Here we see some early members of the tennis club in about 1911.

Market Rasen is well known for three things: its railway station, its racecourse and de Aston School. Here the railway station is having a new roof erected in 1941. Unfortunately the roof was built in a hurry during those hectic war years.

Fiery Sun was the winner of the Wainfleet Selling Handicap Hurdle held at Market Rasen racecourse on 23 September 1989. From left to right are Paul Matthews, John Maltby, *Fiery Sun* (trained by G. Oldroyd), the head lad, John Martin, and Gordon Kirk.

The Market Place, with its pump and cobbles, shows us how Market Rasen differs from Middle Rasen and West Rasen.

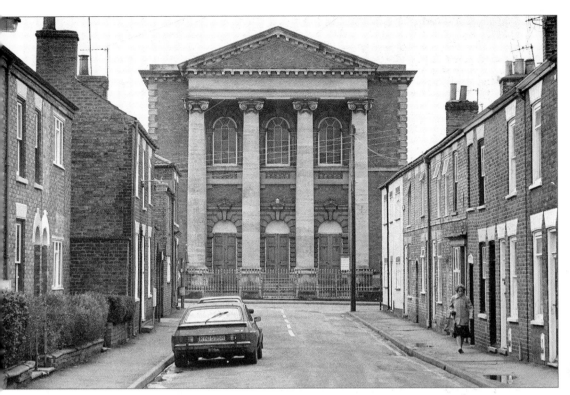

Probably the most impressive chapel still standing in the Wolds is the Centenary Methodist Chapel in Market Rasen. It stands at one end of Union Street, and its neo-classical theme is rather reminiscent of Willingham Hall.

Willingham Hall was the home of the Boucherett family for over a hundred years. Latterly it was used as a training centre by Lindsey Civil Defence Corps before being blown up (like Bayons Manor) in the early '60s.

Arthur Mee described Binbrook in his *King's England – Lincolnshire*: 'The broach spire of the church rising above the trees and the red-pantiled roofs of the houses make an attractive rural picture; and pleasing, too, the little market square, redolent of other days.'

Set in the centre of Binbrook is the Georgian Manor House which was long the family home of the Johnsons and latterly the Clarkes. This back view of the Manor was taken in 1904.

Woodthorpe Johnson Clarke (1856–1916) in between two 'Edwardian Roses' on the tennis court of Binbrook Manor, 1907.

The Clarkes were friendly with the Player family from Nottingham. Here we see Violet Clarke and Mrs Player in 1909.

This unusual photograph shows Edwardian ladies retiring from the garden at Binbrook Manor. Mrs Player is on the extreme right.

When the first car arrived in Binbrook in 1909 it caused quite a stir. As can be seen from the group who greeted the driver (Mr Lunt from Birmingham), it was a momentous occasion.

Eventually, in about 1913, the Clarkes bought their own Model T Ford. It was photographed in the yard of Binbrook Manor. These new-fangled automobiles would threaten those old shire horses that had faithfully ploughed the land for centuries.

Peter Barton, the Binbrook Manor groom, photographed in 1914.

In those heady days of 1913 just before the First World War there was time for a football match. It was a scratch team from Kirmond-le-Mire versus Binbrook with, from left to right, H.W. Clarke, W.J. Clarke, A. Keller, J. Fieldsend, the Revd Mr Smith, Dr Wilkinson, H. Odling, Parsons Wright, C. Fieldsend, Tod Wilkinson, Martin Cust, the Revd Mr Bettison (from Wold Newton) and Tom Haxby.

Binbrook had always had strong connections with the RAF. Here we see an FE2.6 flying over Binbrook in 1917.

A close-up of the bi-plane.

When Lieutenant Noel Parker Dixon (from Christchurch, New Zealand) of the Royal Flying Corps (as it was then) married Miss Dorothy Andrews, daughter of the Revd W. Andrews of Claxby Rectory, in Binbrook parish church, there was considerable local interest. Mr Andrews had been rector of Kelstern for a number of years.

Binbrook Manor was used as a recuperation centre for service personnel. Here we see N.P. 'Dickie' Dixon, Dorothy Dixon, N. Garstin, Mrs Clarke, Geoffrey Bone and Norah Wilkinson. All the men are smoking.

Flyers in particular were always welcome. This was Wing Commander Geoffrey Stephenson who was later killed in America.

There was time for tennis as this group shot shows. In the centre of the photograph is Tim Player, of the Nottingham family firm of John Players tobacco.

Ravendale Hall was built in 1720 as a private family home. For years this house served as a retreat to numerous families, including John Wilson Henry Parkinson, Administrative General of Kenya, who died in Mombasa in 1923. A tablet was erected to him in St Martin's Church, East Ravendale. One of the most notable features of this house was its 'bookroom' or library where tomes lined the walls from floor to ceiling. The Hall has recently been converted into a private nursing home – a fate which many similar houses have had to endure.

Cuxwold Hall was built by Henry Thorold in the middle of the nineteenth century. For many years it was the home of Michael Sleight, whose family amassed a fortune from fishing.

This is a sight that was once only too familiar but which has now gone forever – fighter planes at Binbrook. This photograph was taken on Binbrook's twenty-first anniversary. Since its closure in 1982, the airfield at RAF Binbrook has been used in the making of David Puttnam's film *Memphis Belle*, and its quarters have been sold off as private residences.

These days you are more likely to see a hay loader than an aeroplane on any one of the disused airfields dotted about the county.

On the western spur of the Wolds lies the old Roman town of Caistor. This was the Market Place at the turn of the century.

This later view of the Market Place shows how little Caistor has changed.

One of the oldest houses, built in 1692, shows that Caistor used to be quite an important centre but, as Jack Yates recorded in his *Shell Guide to Lincolnshire*, 'there never seems to be much shopping going on in Caistor and the market square has a depressed aspect.' It is difficult to believe that another poet, Henry Newbolt, attended Caistor Grammar School back in 1873. Sir Henry Newbolt, famous for his 'Play up, play up and play the game', was sent to Caistor Grammar at the age of ten (his father having died in 1866 when Henry Newbolt was four). Anthony Bower, the headmaster of Caistor Grammar, had been his father's old Cambridge tutor and achieved an excellent record of scholarships to Eton and Clifton. In 1878 Henry Newbolt passed his scholarship exam and went to Clifton College, Bristol, where he attended as a day-boy in North Town while his mother lived just around the corner in Worcester Crescent, Clifton. Newbolt's schooling in Lincolnshire has often been overlooked in comparison to that other Victorian denizen, Alfred Lord Tennyson.

Even those travellers who pass through Caistor on their way to Brigg cannot fail to be impressed by some examples of the town's Georgian architecture.

During the Second World War recruits from Caistor readily joined the Home Guard. This photograph was taken in the Rothwell area in about 1943.

Because of the way that Caistor is situated on the side of the Wolds, not only does it have some splendid views but it also makes an excellent toboggan run for children in winter.

Two miles away from Caistor lies Pelham's Pillar, which commemorates the planting of twelve million trees by the first Lord Yarburgh (Charles Anderson Pelham).

It would be very remiss of me to complete a book on the Lincolnshire Wolds and not include a photograph of Brocklesby Hall. This Queen Anne house, which was pruned to its present size after the great fire of 1898, is the home of the Earl of Yarborough. Any man who has enough influence to move the borders of a county, as the present Earl's father did when the short-lived County of Humberside came into force, to include the Brocklesby estate in Lincolnshire rather than Humberside, cannot be excluded.

A typical view of harvesting on the Wolds. Those rolling hills serving as a backcloth make a memorable picture.

Lincolnshire once had many thatched cottages. A typical example is Woodbine Cottage in the centre of South Willingham, situated close to the church of St Martin. It can be seen here on the left of the path. Once part of the Hainton estate, this old stone and thatched cottage (sometimes called 'mud and stud') was sold in 1957 for £70! Formerly a post office and possibly an old bakery, it is now a private residence and one of the few remaining thatched houses on the Lincolnshire Wolds.

ACKNOWLEDGEMENTS

In compiling this book I would like to thank the late James Baildom, Tom Barton, Steven Clarke, Bernard Hallgarth, Paul Matthews, Mrs McConnell, John Nielson and the Welhome Galleries for lending me certain photographs. Once again a special thank you must go to the *Grimsby Evening Telegraph* team of Peter Moore, Peter Craig, Peter Chapman and Janet Longden, without whose help this volume would have been very limp, also to Geoffrey Hardyman and Dr Nicholas Bennett for information, and last, but not least, to Louth Secretarial Services for typing the manuscript so carefully.

BRITAIN IN OLD PHOTOGRAPHS

rystwyth & North Ceredigion
und Abingdon
on
rney: A Second Selection
ng the Avon from Stratford to
 wkesbury
incham
ersham
und Amesbury
lesey
old & Bestwood
old & Bestwood: A Second
 election
ndel & the Arun Valley
bourne
und Ashby-de-la-Zouch
o Aircraft
esbury
am & Tooting
buryshire
nes, Mortlake & Sheen
nsley
consfield
ford
fordshire at Work
worth
erley
ley
eford
con
ningham Railways
op's Stortford &
 wbridgeworth
opstone & Seaford
opstone & Seaford: A Second
 election
k Country Aviation
k Country Railways
k Country Road Transport
kburn
kpool
und Blandford Forum
chley
ton
rnemouth
dford
ntree & Bocking at Work
con
ntwood
dgwater & the River Parrett
llington
port & the Bride Valley
erley Hill
ghton & Hove
ghton & Hove: A Second
 election
tol
und Bristol
xton & Norwood
ly Broadstairs & St Peters
mley, Keston & Hayes

Buckingham & District
Burford
Bury
Bushbury
Camberwell
Cambridge
Cannock Yesterday & Today
Canterbury: A Second Selection
Castle Combe to Malmesbury
Chadwell Heath
Chard & Ilminster
Chatham Dockyard
Chatham & Gillingham
Cheadle
Cheam & Belmont
Chelmsford
Cheltenham: A Second Selection
Cheltenham at War
Cheltenham in the 1950s
Chepstow & the River Wye
Chesham Yesterday & Today
Cheshire Railways
Chester
Chippenham & Lacock
Chiswick
Chorley & District
Cirencester
Around Cirencester
Clacton-on-Sea
Around Clitheroe
Clwyd Railways
Clydesdale
Colchester
Colchester 1940–70
Colyton & Seaton
The Cornish Coast
Corsham & Box
The North Cotswolds
Coventry: A Second Selection
Around Coventry
Cowes & East Cowes
Crawley New Town
Around Crawley
Crewkerne & the Ham Stone
 Villages
Cromer
Croydon
Crystal Palace, Penge & Anerley
Darlington
Darlington: A Second Selection
Dawlish & Teignmouth
Deal
Derby
Around Devizes
Devon Aerodromes
East Devon at War
Around Didcot & the Hagbournes
Dorchester
Douglas
Dumfries
Dundee at Work
Durham People

Durham at Work
Ealing & Northfields
East Grinstead
East Ham
Eastbourne
Elgin
Eltham
Ely
Enfield
Around Epsom
Esher
Evesham to Bredon
Exeter
Exmouth & Budleigh Salterton
Fairey Aircraft
Falmouth
Farnborough
Farnham: A Second Selection
Fleetwood
Folkestone: A Second Selection
Folkestone: A Third Selection
The Forest of Dean
Frome
Fulham
Galashiels
Garsington
Around Garstang
Around Gillingham
Gloucester
Gloucester: from the Walwin
 Collection
North Gloucestershire at War
South Gloucestershire at War
Gosport
Goudhurst to Tenterden
Grantham
Gravesend
Around Gravesham
Around Grays
Great Yarmouth
Great Yarmouth: A Second
 Selection
Greenwich & Woolwich
Grimsby
Around Grimsby
Grimsby Docks
Gwynedd Railways
Hackney: A Second Selection
Hackney: A Third Selection
From Haldon to Mid-Dartmoor
Hammersmith & Shepherd's Bush
Hampstead to Primrose Hill
Harrow & Pinner
Hastings
Hastings: A Second Selection
Haverfordwest
Hayes & West Drayton
Around Haywards Heath
Around Heathfield
Around Heathfield: A Second
 Selection
Around Helston

Around Henley-on-Thames
Herefordshire
Herne Bay
Heywood
The High Weald
The High Weald: A Second
 Selection
Around Highworth
Around Highworth & Faringdon
Hitchin
Holderness
Honiton & the Otter Valley
Horsham & District
Houghton-le-Spring &
 Hetton-le-Hole
Houghton-le-Spring & Hetton-le-
 Hole: A Second Selection
Huddersfield: A Second Selection
Huddersfield: A Third Selection
Ilford
Ilfracombe
Ipswich: A Second Selection
Islington
Jersey: A Third Selection
Kendal
Kensington & Chelsea
East Kent at War
Keswick & the Central Lakes
Around Keynsham & Saltford
The Changing Face of Keynsham
Kingsbridge
Kingston
Kinver
Kirkby & District
Kirkby Lonsdale
Around Kirkham
Knowle & Dorridge
The Lake Counties at Work
Lancashire
The Lancashire Coast
Lancashire North of the Sands
Lancashire Railways
East Lancashire at War
Around Lancaster
Lancing & Sompting
Around Leamington Spa
Around Leamington Spa:
 A Second Selection
Leeds in the News
Leeds Road & Rail
Around Leek
Leicester
The Changing Face of Leicester
Leicester at Work
Leicestershire People
Around Leighton Buzzard &
 Linslade
Letchworth
Lewes
Lewisham & Deptford:
 A Second Selection
Lichfield

Lincoln
Lincoln Cathedral
The Lincolnshire Coast
Liverpool
Around Llandudno
Around Lochaber
Theatrical London
Around Louth
The Lower Fal Estuary
Lowestoft
Luton
Lympne Airfield
Lytham St Annes
Maidenhead
Around Maidenhead
Around Malvern
Manchester
Manchester Road & Rail
Mansfield
Marlborough: A Second Selection
Marylebone & Paddington
Around Matlock
Melton Mowbray
Around Melksham
The Mendips
Merton & Morden
Middlesbrough
Midsomer Norton & Radstock
Around Mildenhall
Milton Keynes
Minehead
Monmouth & the River Wye
The Nadder Valley
Newark
Around Newark
Newbury
Newport, Isle of Wight
The Norfolk Broads
Norfolk at War
North Fylde
North Lambeth
North Walsham & District
Northallerton
Northampton
Around Norwich
Nottingham 1944–74
The Changing Face of Nottingham
Victorian Nottingham
Nottingham Yesterday & Today
Nuneaton
Around Oakham
Ormskirk & District
Otley & District
Oxford: The University
Oxford Yesterday & Today
Oxfordshire Railways: A Second
   Selection
Oxfordshire at School
Around Padstow
Pattingham & Wombourne

Penwith
Penzance & Newlyn
Around Pershore
Around Plymouth
Poole
Portsmouth
Poulton-le-Fylde
Preston
Prestwich
Pudsey
Radcliffe
RAF Chivenor
RAF Cosford
RAF Hawkinge
RAF Manston
RAF Manston: A Second Selection
RAF St Mawgan
RAF Tangmere
Ramsgate & Thanet Life
Reading
Reading: A Second Selection
Redditch & the Needle District
Redditch: A Second Selection
Richmond, Surrey
Rickmansworth
Around Ripley
The River Soar
Romney Marsh
Romney Marsh: A Second
   Selection
Rossendale
Around Rotherham
Rugby
Around Rugeley
Ruislip
Around Ryde
St Albans
St Andrews
Salford
Salisbury
Salisbury: A Second Selection
Salisbury: A Third Selection
Around Salisbury
Sandhurst & Crowthorne
Sandown & Shanklin
Sandwich
Scarborough
Scunthorpe
Seaton, Lyme Regis & Axminster
Around Seaton & Sidmouth
Sedgley & District
The Severn Vale
Sherwood Forest
Shrewsbury
Shrewsbury: A Second Selection
Shropshire Railways
Skegness
Around Skegness
Skipton & the Dales
Around Slough

Smethwick
Somerton & Langport
Southampton
Southend-on-Sea
Southport
Southwark
Southwell
Southwold to Aldeburgh
Stafford
Around Stafford
Staffordshire Railways
Around Staveley
Stepney
Stevenage
The History of Stilton Cheese
Stoke-on-Trent
Stoke Newington
Stonehouse to Painswick
Around Stony Stratford
Around Stony Stratford: A Second
   Selection
Stowmarket
Streatham
Stroud & the Five Valleys
Stroud & the Five Valleys: A
   Second Selection
Stroud's Golden Valley
The Stroudwater and Thames &
   Severn Canals
The Stroudwater and Thames &
   Severn Canals: A Second
   Selection
Suffolk at Work
Suffolk at Work: A Second
   Selection
The Heart of Suffolk
Sunderland
Sutton
Swansea
Swindon: A Third Selection
Swindon: A Fifth Selection
Around Tamworth
Taunton
Around Taunton
Teesdale
Teesdale: A Second Selection
Tenbury Wells
Around Tettenhall & Codshall
Tewkesbury & the Vale of
   Gloucester
Thame to Watlington
Around Thatcham
Around Thirsk
Thornbury to Berkeley
Tipton
Around Tonbridge
Trowbridge
Around Truro
TT Races
Tunbridge Wells

Tunbridge Wells: A Second
   Selection
Twickenham
Uley, Dursley & Cam
The Upper Fal
The Upper Tywi Valley
Uxbridge, Hillingdon & Cowley
The Vale of Belvoir
The Vale of Conway
Ventnor
Wakefield
Wallingford
Walsall
Waltham Abbey
Wandsworth at War
Wantage, Faringdon & the Vale
   Villages
Around Warwick
Weardale
Weardale: A Second Selection
Wednesbury
Wells
Welshpool
West Bromwich
West Wight
Weston-super-Mare
Around Weston-super-Mare
Weymouth & Portland
Around Wheatley
Around Whetstone
Whitchurch to Market Drayton
Around Whitstable
Wigton & the Solway Plain
Willesden
Around Wilton
Wimbledon
Around Windsor
Wingham, Addisham &
   Littlebourne
Wisbech
Witham & District
Witney
Around Witney
The Witney District
Wokingham
Around Woodbridge
Around Woodstock
Woolwich
Woolwich Royal Arsenal
Around Wootton Bassett,
   Cricklade & Purton
Worcester
Worcester in a Day
Around Worcester
Worcestershire at Work
Around Worthing
Wotton-under-Edge to Chipping
   Sodbury
Wymondham & Attleborough
The Yorkshire Wolds

To order any of these titles please telephone our distributor, Littlehampton Book Services on 01903 72159
For a catalogue of these and our other titles please ring Regina Schinner on 01453 731114